ON

A

STAIR

ANN

LAUTERBACH

On

A

Stair

PENGUIN POETS

PENGUIN BOOKS
Published by the Penguin Group
Penguin Putnam Inc., 375 Hudson Street,
New York, New York 10014, U.S.A.
Penguin Books Ltd, 27 Wrights Lane, London W8 5TZ, England
Penguin Books Australia Ltd, Ringwood, Victoria, Australia
Penguin Books Canada Ltd, 10 Alcorn Avenue,
Toronto, Ontario, Canada M4V 3B2
Penguin Books (N.Z.) Ltd, 182-190 Wairau Road,
Auckland 10, New Zealand

Penguin Books Ltd, Registered Offices:
Harmondsworth, Middlesex, England

First published in Penguin Books 1997

10 9 8 7 6 5 4 3 2

LIBRARY OF CONGRESS CATALOGING IN PUBLICATION DATA
Lauterbach, Ann, 1942–
    On a stair/Ann Lauterbach.
      p.   cm.—(Penguin poets)
    ISBN 0 14 058.793 4 (pbk.)
    I. Title.
PS3562.A84405   1997
811'.54—dc21   97-3564

Printed in the United States of America
Set in Bembo

For Nan Graham
For Peter and Susan Straub

Grateful acknowledgment is made to the editors of the following journals, in which some of the poems in this collection (many in earlier drafts) were first published:

Avec: "Poem of the Landscape," "Sequence with Dream Objects in Real Time"; *Bomb*: "N/est"; *The Colorado Review*: "The Return of Weather"; *Conjunctions*: "Blake's Lagoon"; *Denver Quarterly*: "Figure without Ground"; *Gulf Coast*: "Staircase"; *The Iowa Review*: "Bramble Portrait"; *The Kenyon Review*: "Nocturnal Reel"; *New American Writing*: "A Valentine for Tomorrow," "Daylight Savings Time," "Free Fall," "Poise on Row," "Delayed Elegy."

"Invocation" was first published as part of a portfolio for Bernadette Mayer by The Figures Press.

"A Clown, Some Colors, A Doll, Her Stories, A Song, A Moonlit Cove" was published as a book in a collaboration with artist Ellen Phelan by the Library Fellows of the Whitney Museum of American Art. It was subsequently published as an issue of *Abacus*.

NOTE

Gratitude to: Courtney Hodell and Paul Slovak for their care at Penguin; Peter Straub, Heather Ramsdell, Stacy Doris, and Joan Richardson for their readings; Caroline Chinlund for her listening; and, as always, to my students for their going on.

I am grateful, once again, to the John D. and Catherine T. MacArthur Foundation and to the Corporation of Yaddo, for the gift of protected liberty.

The question "where is the thing?" is inseparable from the question "where is the human?" Like the fetish, like the toy, things are not properly anywhere, because their place is found on this side of objects and beyond the human in a zone that is no longer objective or subjective, neither personal nor impersonal, neither material nor immaterial, but where we find ourselves suddenly facing these apparently simple unknowns: the human, the thing.

—GIORGIO AGAMBEN

Where now? Who now? When now? Unquestioning. I, say I. Unbelieving. Questions, hypotheses, call them that. Keep going, going on, call that going, call that on.

—SAMUEL BECKETT

CONTENTS

A Valentine for Tomorrow   *1*

Nocturnal Reel   *4*

Bramble Portrait   *7*

Figure without Ground   *9*

Poem of the Landscape   *11*

On (Tower)   *17*

Night Barrier   *18*

Poise on Row   *21*

Sequence with Dream Objects in Real Time   *23*

Blake's Lagoon   *26*

Free Fall   *29*

On (Word)   *31*

On (Open)   *33*

A Clown, Some Colors, A Doll, Her Stories, A Song, A Moonlit Cove   *34*

On (Thing)   *51*

On (Dream)   *53*

The Return of Weather   *54*

Staircase   *59*

A History Lesson   *61*

Daylight Savings Time   *62*

Delayed Elegy   *64*

And The Question Of   *65*

Poem with Last Line from Epictetus   *68*

Here/This/There/That   *70*

Auction   *72*

On   *75*

N/est   *76*

Invocation   *85*

On
a
Stair

A VALENTINE FOR TOMORROW

1.

Capable as this, where only moments ago

we were in a generation (captive

    (precedent soothing its path—the bad joke, the blunder—

having spent these days in an addition of fears

        (layers, telling it this way

whereas the flair (rhetoric of a bird) had come so far to ease

      forget reference, it burdens the noise *hey we just wanted to*

change the

      old enough to know better

              and so a future which is not the far

        the other coast

    singing

          (awake all night and the

thing wants to

      arrest)

   that was a memory of sorts so forget it

           how can we be news?

           win, lose

we have this couplet

the rhyme is under the nest

and under that is

private.

2.

Boxed in furthest containment, troved, methodic

in range to get there from here

play a tune to your guests they might hum along

might sing take off your clothes be nude

make your heart visible as in a painting heart-shaped

recall the hand touching the skull

the luminous mouth calling *blue*

step of feet on cool tiles dancing

put on your wings fly

out of range into the storm

pluck out the splinter, bleed

the tree will reveal long grains

flowers subside

there will be a dusting of spices and the scent again of the stairwell

toss your rings to the alchemical wind

the rampant vehicle of jest

the blunt gargoyle

will limp out from the blizzard

carve its face in snow, now shall pass now

in a glittering parade

and the mobile digressive figments collide

legacy of heavens where darkly dressed figures scavenge for stars.

3.

But I know a way
where the ligature of morning is even with the stars and
before that, on occasion, off and on into Friday, whose voice is the voice
—nocturnal reverie without the captured dove. What you say, how I adhere
so prayer comes ghostlike and erudite
into the coffin's partition, and the unanimous speech of angels—
their incomplete test. Light in the window (a quotation) is how we notice
discrepancy—*hello, hello, I forget*—incendiary fuel
tearing roof from house, rats from dream,
acquiescent cloth draped over the little town's vocabulary:

If I sweep all the streets will you hold the dustpan?
If I fly to the moon will you watch?
If I send you a book will you press the petals?
If I tell you I'm cold will you uncover my heart?

Adrift under the forgotten speech of our halcyon days when the club
met down by the sea and graduated at dawn in pink dresses,
when the pavement was good for walking
toward a park, in spring
there was spring then pinned to the pillow of a girl
asleep on the surface, her hair scented with it, ringed
with desire. *I dare you* is what we said
to the old god drunk as a skunk at the bar
as the obligatory craft of strangers rattled the cage.
Out all night visiting the tide as it swept over the city's rapture—
ritual drum answering, turning to steam by morning.
Now we could see a normal oracle blinking and cruel
humming a tune on the boardwalk—

If I swallow your seed will it fill me?
If I follow your lead will it kill me?

and a child with a pail and some sand and some glue.

NOCTURNAL REEL

Denouncing or affirming, their vison fed on the distance
between promise and fact.
—Sacvan Bercovitch, *The American Jeremiad*

She saw that setting was everything she could know, but that
its cause was stupendous and wretched. Everything
required her gaze, as if that alone could repair it.
Across the evening a man on a bicycle poured by
and this seemed an emblem of time racing—the acute thing
manifest and then gone, like a brute song in an unknown language
summoning all to drill. A residual tune kept playing until
it fell into a compost of notes
mouldering in the fields, taken up here and there
by morning's adrift gleam, as if caught
on nettle, bright noise of birds,
dull flit of petals fallen on blue stone.

And whatever constellations thus begun, freestanding
in occupied territory—*25,000 objects*
made by craftsmen, admission free,
soil peeled away like skin—all this
changed, exchanged into that.

                And whatsoever is begun—
on her knees, framed
above and below
contusion in her mouth
flawed into saying
                   (a still arrow
                          falls
               under the wound
                         (another
          partition (picture's aporia, metaphorical gash
            gaunt precipice of the near

(early, earliest ground

                lilac ash

           broken urn

       summoned from the truant by the guide

back on track

       (the plan to build an extension

    lethal map

angle of descent

staircase.

In such streaks of riot
she forgets the object
to wander to create a vacancy to forget
and drops a stitch.
Was there a body wrapped in a canopy? Things
happened within it, thorns migrated
at the wrist as if sealed,
closely watched, a boy's collection of soldiers
marched on the kitchen tarp.

        I detaches

enters the disparate pool

          The carpet
          The cup
          The cello
          The gun
          The bracelet

It was (as if

    a slight memory of wet pine, thunder

      immobile overhead

        she had forgotten to say

        and so scattered

        one by one

            for omission, for delay

     so that weapons hung overhead

                                in a bouquet

                                                        (as if bequeathed
                                (as if her hands held an infant's head
                                                dead bird in eaves

decomposing
the familial nest.
(Not) being thrown
into care, the bloods scatter

                                Garden)garden
                                        stone cast into her mouth
                                                (under the knife)
                                                        layered leaves, their

green resemblances, their
difficult spots
destined to go a little way down the path.

Silence prowls
so that the mind of the listener begins to wander
under the canopy of what has been said
which is only night consuming itself,
iteration by iteration, into silt. Confession
drags biography into view like a saint briefly captured
in a photograph: blurred image of her smile, flames
cascading upwards into sample perdition—sacrificial,
sacrifice always naked, as if just minted, as a star is minted by night.
She places herself there, in music's pocket, temporal glee
restored, tale told, deed released
thru an opening
the way a flower, despite all watching, opens.
Is this voice—remnant hum of the living,
message replayed—sufficient? Will this syntax
keep (forbidden or preserved) promise from fact?

BRAMBLE PORTRAIT

Stunned under legacies of a statue's respite
stitched light
boldly faced, facsimile's ghost
held up
not yet unleashed and
you/the child
              comes to say
                 this inscription, this
solid state
        variable in the garden, the memory of one evening, or
the trip resisted
(who names it forgets its name)
        and the dream shows
            a picture held forth as phantom
        (which it cannot
          and is never really so)
                    What is that?

      Here I comes
bewitched by the pregnant field
the undressed moon
song–stripped, its
ancient insignias
rinsed, contractions riveted to heat's
withdrawal from the garden floor

cutout leaves dripping ink
postcards brilliantly unsent.

Forgotten in rapid transition
the street's drone goes
go go

I

shifts tableaux, her
eyes close and the cerulean evening
is flat, laid far under the pillow

coins, dragon, bell,
one-armed monk,
painted Russian egg,
blackboard under rose storm, girl
sitting among crumbs and dry petals, hair uplifted,
a cock, pinfeathers erect, the delicate lineage of a kiss.

In an insatiable cancellation the figures
are refuted, their histories
burdened, façades musically transgressed.
How can reason reflect water? How
can the swimming child come up for air, her mouth intact?
Had we not said *the drink, the beautiful, the bright today?*
Look! Morning stampedes inarticulate shade
into a caress, loosely
constrained, variable and same,
moving along the timeline,
along the threshold of a ledge—
whole of any sky, side of a building
coated in ochre paint, wedding dress netting lost air—
now leased to awe's precarious delay
whose appearance is only dawn
clutching at night's *flit flit flit*
against the elegy's insidious decorum,
not yet counted among the day's inequities.

FIGURE WITHOUT GROUND

No more than a woman with her umbrella
heading outside, resisting bad weather
　　　　　　　　　　　—Bei Dao

1.

The bridge spans these puddles.
A red chair faces bricks, white curtains
open onto the trek, steepled shadows drape over the city,
dust cloths billow, bodies in protective garb,
illegible scrawl across yellow trucks.
And a scent of jasmine and sandalwood while Susanna,
reflected in patches, sings.
Where did you say history is? Here?
At this intersection, in this lot, with this noise
rammed into morning, or the talk
in a room with strangers, one
hunched in a pit, child
digging to China, printed
page, description of scene, drunk woman,
Dollhouse Depot, Purple Turtle Lounge,
Dead People's Things,
this silver ring kept in a box, that dome's surcease, mysterious
illness, red alert, bride's dress—
Mom, what's for dinner?

2.

How to emerge from the chrysalis,
recover from the shopping cart's
cinematic rampage

bring the child
onto high country near wooded peaks
a long time ago, so long ago as to be only once,
out of this story
into indigo dawn—
canyons of mordant dye
small rusty trees
        onto the empty agora
           apprehension miraged as an Umbrella of infinite dilation
              incidental Arc
                    spanned over nothing—

birds return, drafting the future
like innocent bystanders.

3.

Or, immobile,
crumpled in
stain
rubbed into the robe's
hooded stasis, sheen
of a door
sealed to the last
night's certainty open to us
as neon dots transcribing the sanctuary
fall into space
and you, holy or damned, ride from from the observable canvas
and I, the lament, turn back

unencumbered by what might be said of the event.

POEM OF THE LANDSCAPE

Prevalent spinning. High winds. Foothills. One red light
pulses the western way—
Ace of Into the Night, Ace of Hearts—
and the boxes are emptied of their visiting. But the complete works are
apocryphal—*Says, says,* a person speaks against odds, as in a cage.

The day, unresisting, webs running malls
with white hair, and a cat. Alley
without memory, only pails, surging plastic, the last of all stories,
the blasted parts, what the classics held, what is forgotten of them.
But the language of the fence lures
an unfettered brisk
motion of turning, to turn
the caravan into a circle. *Dear Mother: the earth here*
upheaves into monstrous beauty
we cannot pass. The exhausted geese
doodle in low air, their arrow
disheveled to a scrawl. Everything is for sale today, every harness
and glove, each misgiving, every simile aroused by a map.
The sky is black with receipts.
What have we done, but gamble
the stray profits of our
quest? Iconographies of dread
pilfer an insatiable ghost; an artless bell
strikes again arcane renunciations. Slender facets of the *chanteuse*
linger, her neck exposed
to the earnest American desert, to which
the Black Dog howls.
Maven of Circumference, your season is
here, in the pitched peaks, the dry conundrum of attic calendars—
cold perfume, birds trapped in eaves.
In the far window your double rose, and went
into banishment of a neuter heaven.

Cycling pigeons thieve the light
and tear it to shredded reparations
as if the angelic were confetti's
scrap, a continuum of strokes
through whose wide incursions they and all else
fall into a heap of artifacts
hauled to the next coast, betraying
what was not said in response.

                    Could speak to the palm
                to the lame
         could have no drift could lie among
                     could leave could put could steal
                          the architecture's pale stone could
        hear snow sift into cloud could touch the object's journey
        converse with the toy with the speed with wheels along the way
        could be trailing their names could call to them could ask
        could laugh inside the story could motion to them to sit down
        could deny could allow cease repeating distances could be excessive cry
        be without bring forth could lean down
        could kiss could lick could envelop
        count resemble be dressed accordingly could deny
        hold up to the light give details
        could be ashamed
        could ponder could pave
        instill decide assemble flaunt agree

          Men find their wardrobes, the sleeves or selves fit.
Were this before dawn, we might know why they thumb through rags, folding each
at the rip. Their cart has squeaky wheels, carrying the sky
like a painted ceiling's redundancy, Apollo's curve
across the chariot's beaded way
connecting one star to another,

east to west to east. Now
a phantom child's abbreviation
unlocks the grave at the ground's
material zone as the world, opening, begins to imitate
a chalice.

And then space was carved into acres;
bowls passed from hand to hand, seeds were planted into the fields' affirmation,
one thing after another: arrangement, way, tool. Birdsong and the
swish of traffic, voice of objects animating the filmic infestation
into semantic glue, the binding along the spine, windows and pages trim.

Are you? she asks, or *Will you?*
as she drops a penny into her father's slot, watches the ocean turn,
cherries spin into flame, igniting the desert with festival. And so she dances with a
shadow of an arcane dove. The staircase spirals upward tracing the
curve of desire; clowns, hooligans and slippered minions take up their post,
giggling into the wet theater; gnomes sweep muddied prints; lacy herbs are
strewn, some poisonous, some not.

Lurid, haphazard,
decorated with dew, a dossier
begins to fill. Gates
form, and migratory shapes, mutable as embers.
Under the logo of a furnace the collections spread.

Cryptic Snail
why dost thou dally on
frozen rock?

What Spiral trail
spews its print
on ice

coat of ebbtide
needle point
jetty in sand

love
spinning wheels
spitting glue

Serpent of Night
what is this zero
to what is it fixed?

Her function, the purpose of
her journey, is to

ask any question, *What is the grass? Have you seen
my socks?*

Two pails, one green, one brown, are empty. A third, black with a
three painted on it in large white handwriting, at a distance of some yards—

the man who found the soiled bookbag

is gone

single tree now a pole

Is this the Inspection Place?

1. Whip
2. Inspection Place
3. W3
4. hat/boot
5. Doubts confusions
6. (Let's go)
7. Help
8. (What was I saying)
9. Sky
10. Sleep
11. (Remembering)
12. approach by stages
13. Divisions
14. Lighting

The friction of the Given accosts our lens; dawn
papers over a skeletal real, a truce is made
with its folds. It could be early after all.
Sliding open her veil, Help
strides into view
like the portrait of a Beautiful Girl
in white garments, holding a hat.
Is this the fiction needed to pull us onto the street,
onto the rug sliding along the excavated path, wherein the Spider nests
and the catechism of belief?

                              In a cluster of meanwhiles

we wait. The white coat recedes, balding
and deleting limbs, rooftops, swaying
network of wires. Meanwhile
a white car
drives slowly across the city
like time's target

and the seraphic wing at the periphery
stretches
over the horizon
where a blue thread
pulls the unpicturing spool
whose river leaves Eden

           their amazed stare
citizens
of the rite weaving flimsy reeds
across the whole carcass of Embodied Cause.
Perpetual goad, could this She
have failed, turning
toward the grassy carpet, inscribed with the magic
of the plains, shards of found delight, scrolls
of indecipherable measure, striped dye
traveling into the loom's fret of desire?

What made her hand reach
mated there
to his frame, the rhyming
design of their advent out of Name into Condition?
The enameled sky is a
floor over which shadows
sweep resemblances—profile of his head, muscular
indentations of her back, wild projecting thong
or tusk threading up into the night's cavern,
nomadic cipher of an enflamed sword.
Necessary Story, why did you begin?

to Bin Ramke

ON (Tower)

Big snow, little snow is what the Indians
say, and the gray
turned yellow and you followed it
to the tower with ice house below,
prayer room above. The big snow
slowly fell. Someone had found
a remnant ecclesiastical carpet
to lay on the stairs. *Last year,* he said,
I was not the same as now
that my sister is dead, my father dying.
And you wanted to know
what to make of the snake-eating man
on the far side of an island
where the song, a prelude to everything we tell,
began. And you wanted to know why,
in the yellow light, gangs form to extinguish it.

to Elizabeth Rubin

17

NIGHT BARRIER

Men assemble in a trussed league
whose least crime is not known

foot after favorite foot whose biography
is quoted

    at the gate

of the subject.
Three into three goes ?

Last things first, and the itching contusion
of accident *(after chance rolled thru)*—he said

something about a monkey and lo!
it appeared on the unguarded screen

confirming

Logos

  into library and our aspiration

black
mark on the white

present, to present

an age
shrunk to a stipend or clock.
There must be, if there must be

obsidian halo
grassy knoll

over in the contingent dream
historical marker
this not knowing is not a lacuna

grassy halo
obsidian knell

three men in blue shirts smiling
their modest affirmation
workers

in pursuit of
another possibility

haunted
by the swerve

the crisis and feast
fatal response

to dust
like an idea of dust

angelic, atomic

        whose shadow moves from hand to mouth

           filling its motion

with infiltration, a thing
whose imprecation swallows
the ground on which it strides, a paltry ghost's
birth.

Change me, it calls, into
substance, a home, garden overlooking a vista,
blossoms, a path, the sea
wherein practice is performed
as the twilight's
confession: Father, I am deliberately
missing the events
by which time is told.
I refuse nourishment, I am
an old woman
ranting on a stoop.

The girl is always dancing behind the leaves.
The fish are always swimming on the screen.

POISE ON ROW

Look laminated dichotomy/field
sutured to field
open your mouth an ocean is within
chronic diaspora
                open open

tribulations of a   *say aint*
                   dust star
                         pollinates

centuries of dew.

And were we to anoint these commodious villages
the eagle would be

high over the perfect V
                         vintage/voyage   hell's mermeronic clip
                             in the glaze of meaning's cup
its logo
itching to be born.

Prudence and Wisdom calypso thru the dark wood, overtly
semantic, while we on trial
obey the moon's hooded grief
whose October is sentenced.

The fool is enticed.
There it is, the display itself,
her nude retreat across the carpet, fictive and mean
as Hopper's vulgate.

What we see is the custodian's lament
—vile Hermes, vile trolling Spirit
raided with alarms

arms relented into an easy clasp
iterated on the path of the prey
as the mock angel, shadow's lilting encumbrance,
feathers his nest.

Just here you might find the gregarious animosity of sorrow
sworn to duality. The tongue
is forked, lathered with desire
and printed thus, and the spin or pin
hits the old heel

          there is a hand held
              the thumb anchors
                 in a torn book
                    and this thumping god
                       stammers across the threshold

    blu

    pur

gre

um wu

  songdirt

    in mir

      in or

        mar

          to market to market

          sayeth the rag.

Paradise is stranged
and the net quenches.

SEQUENCE WITH DREAM OBJECTS
IN REAL TIME

Meandering lit space/chained
mystique of the opulent, now narrow, now culled
as keel or knoll, the uneven crest
over such river decisions
pointing to a narrative chain—second instance of the emblem
wholly uncontained in reverence
of what, now culled, now
recalled, the subject
as particular as eddying knowledge
without its little musical notes/spark of the delicate hand
reduced to

wind's terms
frightened abundance
o that house, that incident
some significant equation (
had we heard? one: the death, two: the repeated
phantasm's

meandering lit space/chained

as the keel or knoll, the uneven crest
over such rivers

uncontained reverence

recalled, the subject
as particular as eddying knowledge

reduced

to frightened abundance

o that house, that incident
some significant equation (
had we heard?

now narrow, now culled

pointing to a narrative chain—second instance of the emblem
in reverence
now
recalled, the subject

without its delicate hand
o that house, that incident
some significant equation (
had we heard? one: the

meandering lit chain
the mystique
as the keel's uneven
river decisions
pointing to a narrative chain—second instance of the emblem
wholly in reverence
of what, now
called the subject,
as particular as eddying knowledge
with musical notes/spark of the delicate hand
reduced to

wind's
frightened abundance
o that house, that incident
some significant equation (
had we heard? one: the death, two: the repeated
phantasm's
frail body flared
down slope, head over

heels, a paper acrobat cartwheeling
down wind, making the skittery sound of things
in wind. And then
in obeisance
turned into an avenue, its
skin peeled into sight's
lesson, the trust that retrieval—
some hand, some eye—will fetch it back
to meaning's chance

night crowded into a
black bag left
near the third rail, giving my sister the pearls,
staring at the map framed in polished burl and now
the wide smiling face
smiling into some width or necessity
this is the   they have
(chained the soldiers) chained (to the door) the door.

BLAKE'S LAGOON

Here rendered
below the rim

going down
under the silence

where the eyes of dawn
seek the eyes of dusk

something like that
blinking

the mutable screen
lingering

     (sun, more sun, so much sun
          it must be a porch of

                    renovated time
              the longest string held across centuries
            an extended drop
      desperate altar
        nave shimmied into least zenith
        unpaginated, balanced

) was it a curve or
      a telescopic dot saying good-bye in
the rain/I think it was a
figure musically witnessed, weather, your face, object
indigenous and unremarked

As if
    to re-vision

providence

     redeem erroneous Providence

the delusory rainbow
a covenant that gives birth
the Shadowy Female whose garments are garments

          milky pearl, clouds of blood

     The place of her protection
surrounded by limbs
delusory covenant

       (blank)

who announces the message which
mirrors her journey
        the Eagle of Prophecy calling
the lovers, the contraries
to view their
embrace
at the edge of the *sea of time and space* (not
a Death Couch, unbound

     sexual garments into *Human Lineaments.*

I will empty this dish
Time has no name for it
it will not grow
made of glossy air

     materials as if plangent or spread
       where the tangles rivet sound into fan shapes

     Will we ever get out of here?

The corner's triangular glass
affixed to an object
(how these visions thwart passage from bed to bed
one honored, one
              by light) deleted.

FREE FALL

More comes along to sustain *flap flap* a departure
this much is uncertain in the wreckage of Verdi

or why asks the girl to her self (looks at now)
voice of the tenor currents of opus

the handheld child mentioned in passing
day on its side too many pages

turning *if then* flat as a five
numerical exposure every thing countless

plus evocations plus seedlings plus fish
among ingredients where a kiss leaves its mark

translating habitude to the rash on the throat
incidental flight no less than free fall

Source of the whose of why of when
what map travels what speed what incentive

incidental expression then a career
o dally awhile off the expedient trail

gather a myth from the unused archive
save a place at the stop (wave to the camera)

bring some white twice as big as an orchid
the spoils of a wish the path of a snag

arrange to meet at the edge of a lip
did you smile in your sleep did you order this

beast or trigger (hand under belt)
what did he say at the close of night

among the epithets permanent (sequestered)
(could not be found) bracket our sequel

sock lost on the rug target of ruin
city of haloes of exits of sorts

flap flap the dragon I thought it was Sunday
at least it was under the ambush of evening

fetch me a braid the stairs are they open?
speak not to strangers they covet your tongue.

ON (Word)

O but the sky! unhinged *junket junket*
traverse Perpetua the jays, the trucks—
these are violent times
and our songs are old.
Hast seen a ghost? Hast fled a tree
collapsing on your head? And the snow rushes.
And the storm passes.
Are we mere vocabularies?
I do or do not believe in God.
She does or does not love him.
He did or did not commit a crime.
The hairy-armed man is dressed
in the flowered frock of his second-grade teacher—
A Mrs. Flood from Columbus. He carries
a large shiny handbag, a gun, a camera
to record their vacation on the east coast.
He is or is not a woman.
Words turn on the mischief of their telling.

ON (Open)

Sheaf or sheet or sheer (hearing
a turn closer than
an island, proportion of mind
as a circle (sorrow comes round
voracious and pungent
girl meets boy the waiting emblem
geography's spirit (too close to count)
and a hint of mercy in the weeds, the goodly weeds,
the wand of the keeper
(circus in town, hand of a stranger)
weighted tents open to all.
Nothing is optional. Nothing closed.

A CLOWN, SOME COLORS,
A DOLL, HER STORIES, A SONG,
A MOONLIT COVE

1.

Ur said Clown from a shelf said Harmony Clown
from his seat on the shelf before Is

ur ur said Clown, repeating the said

> from a dusty
> green bike

> from
> a thicket of
> keys
> a dump under

> clover
> from kiss

from the Tale of a Tub, an awful color
an unhealed lump

from the Dwelling of Dwellings
ur our Urn said Migrating Clown.

Is this field's dementia, its prow?
I am thirsty in the aisle
in the shallow preambled space
below this whatnot sheet
above that rusty brow.

Am I safe or for sale?
asked Clown from his crib.
Do I have a use? he inquired.
Will I fall will fly is there
a bridge or a sill?
There's a rose on my nose, said Clown.

        The laws are erased/I cannot see from this echo

     the locked port and grimy window/I think I saw
     boughs with few innoculators/air was not part of

that scene/I am missing
part of my throat/my mouth jumps

Am I lost or stolen? Did I belong to a thing?
Did I live in a tent or a stream?
Are these eyes borrowed? (they seem to be used)
Did I once have a sex? Is it this?

2.

A coin caught in a bramble like a tear in hair

        This would be Silver

An arrow or error/no marks
reef dismantled/pearls
roll under ebb tides

     mercurial tracks scalded

        This would be Yellow

I am made of newsprint and milk
my feet and hands are wax

I have no boots to hike thru Jerusalem

This would be Black

I am in need of stilts
in need of transition
something to follow/a wall to dismantle/gauze for my head

This would be Green

Please find me a thread near the river
a ribbon for my throat
Is this hope in my cup or a sock?

This would be Red

Incessantly stripped world must I enter
your chamber/I live in the morning's attic

Am I poor or wise?
Am I awake?
Am I bride or nun?
What is fun?
I know I am strange and fake.

Must I go to the spot where the man is?
I'd rather not

This would be White

3.

The party folds, finds its coil.
After such, a pattern of such.
A third is needed, coins for change.

Illegible me
crater under a sky heap.
Coins for turning from the inexact.

Dancing out there on the rim
enthusiasm among shy animals.
Remedy of the solution, however inexact.

Leaving out a day, and another day
a poison is about to be swallowed.
A solution in bright water.

Prim armature, and the belly
coming undone in exaggerated formats.
Snow to water, water to mist.

Watch. Whatever could we watch?
An accident televised? A rebellion?
We missed the final episode, the revenge.

Not blamed because
the incident was not recorded.
Revenge over coffee, the sweet good-bye.

Farewell, holy one.
May the exit be deft and merry.
Goodbye, goodbye.

4.

Afternoon's misguided handle
dangles on itself and beyond.

Laughter is the remedy, he said
from decorum's permanent cage.

Yet the tree, the tree doesn't laugh.
What is that bending and giggling?

It's a heart in a field of hearts
trying to pry open the locked jaw of air.

A cast of thousands newly installed
in a democratic regime.

An iterating mirage,
the what for which we search.

And the new bloom in the window box?
That too is red, but is kept behind bars.

It's a parade, he said
from under the annals of greed.

5.

Fled, said Doll, eyeing
the shadow of a shoe.

What leaps? What falls?
Is noon cast off?

Not yet blooming as aftermath,
sequence stunned in a bud

a blush of erasures, of prints.
Someone, not me, was here

dreaming of day, as of
inclusion.

One shoe hopped away.
(If what opens fails to open

is it asleep?)
This does not fit.

Outside, is it infinite
or just dark?

6.

The solitary design is not inherited.
It says of itself *shadow, veil, shadow*

inventing a smile in the mirror
with pink lights. It has eyes

because the child sees herself
as an oval tracing

disguise after disguise, her
picture and merit.

     Under a reprieve
      an orchid

innuendo

upscale as flotsam on a hearth
breathes innuendo

and a collection of meanwhiles
ravenous for more

filters thru
the quotidian spray

scented by
pathology of an adventure
its lesions

in Paradise.

The children are weeping
the dear one is afraid to come home

to the rage of material
laid out in print

an opening
not to be shut

by any such kisses
or the rags of the twisted clock.

Berserk in artifacts
he continues to pray.

And the mirror
is inside the house inside the mirror.

There is observation of the sky
from there, although the curtains are closed

as if winter.
Winter in cause after cause, each

held by a clasp, a
hook and eye, a row of small

pearl buttons with thongs,
their crescent nails

the milky sheen
of old porcelain—

hairline webbings,
leaks. That night

a single candle gave forth its meager scent
and the lovers sat staring into it

as the trough of water
rocked gently—

hypothetical desire
cast in real wax.

7.

Unremitting architecture of trust.

8.

The Book of Hanging Gardens.

9.

Visits to Zoos and Sanctuaries.

10.

Once I knew a Tree
in an episode of doing
it was a lesson in leaving
I did not learn.
 Among my friends much is forgotten.
Once, in a crowd, there was
fool's gold, oceans of musk,
awful procedures,
cold dung.
I cruised there
in ample foraging hunger.
Black nets over beasts
enormous as mountains
swift as elevators.
Big jokes above the city.
Arcane paths or patches
and food, hot food, for scholars.
Is this a circus or a cloud? I asked,
watching the cast of lights
in the sky.
VA
and *vA*
and *variation* said the sequel
blowing its tune into vapors
political and dumb.
Without attachment a riot.
Even a Clown knows that.

11.

Silver ship
           darns under the moon, severs a little mercy.
Some gifts were left above the meadow
they are
storied in the picture
they are a tune in the sun *the ugly sun.*
Some gifts where the young are laughing, tearing themselves into
small trinkets, into
clipping knots. And up there is speech
with a smudge, the dirty hand of the night
harming its mouth. Now it will never say *yes*
never say *Hi, this is*
my music in a box
this is my hand reaching into a pocket for keys.
It wants to sit up, make it sit up!
It wants to sleep, sing it to sleep.

Lullaby of the Moon

The floor gathers an unseemly rate
obituary or fortress *(fate)*

spine of fields
finality or spindle *(yields)*

beautiful endurance
royal furl of the carpet *(dance)*

on each cusp a dove
on each palm a grove *(love)*

wherefore she hangs her home
from a string, from hair *(comb)*

last fling of domain
faultless cove *(rain)*

carrying a city within
fine tool of belonging *(skin)*

demeanor of the lost
side by side in the arch *(cost)*

your king, my flame
ascending to silvers *(name)*

and steady as a hand's reach
where the river is *(teach)*

inhale the dawn
it carries your every pore *(spawn)*

12.

Sleep, mute pietà

flame of sorrow it would say
into silent thunder

                  so the heart
under a cotton chamber
parked under gray loam

        —away swift Orion trailing his belt in the pond
               —away haggard dim sisters
           —away Andromeda sipping mountain mist

stops

raggedy raggedy
bachelor with broken hair

gracious avatar
turned from the entrance

no fear of the slender doll with gold rings at her waist
thighs taut as sails

no fear of the stench of a hand
sheathed in cruelty

the puppeteer's fingers
guiding the weapon, the lance.

Turn, beloved face
to where the mask is unmade

(Joe and Jane married on Saturday
agleam with it)

and two boys
swim toward each other

such fine eyes

                    such finesse—

As in the quantum delirium of a toy god, rushing into captivity
white engine on a screen seeded with
hooped wings gesticulating, wheels rapid as vermin
in last flight, from whence the saints came one by one
to the celebrity camp to dip their eyes in clover.

Hey, Moat Man, have you no nickels, no game
to foil our figures, to
salvage our estimates? This naked thumb
has for its integer *abstain*, has
for its food *suck*. Will you close my eyes?
Will you shave my pelt? In this auditorium
we are an offering, a crust, a pitter and patter
you cannot mimic.

The cliff is
Greek where I go
with large hands, my embrace
(pray that the road is long,
full of adventure, full of knowledge)
tidal in effigy/tallow ebbed from the heart/cut at the heel.
Biographical incision, I will see the very garden
you intended to plant.
Angel of Time, are you so absent
I must trade this shelter for that?

Nest in a rock slit, unfledged creature
cast upon sand.

Witness no Voice.

ON (Thing)

And then having to hide under the thing
the rubber cone or tent
at the foot of a virulent tree
and then she, in Paris, with her hair newly cut
leaving on a train for some place else
and I unable to decide
stranded at the deception
among strange shoes
and the dull ornaments of a regime.
The amber light of the mother is
thickly spread, and patches of carpet
shag green
planted on the sidewalk
to imitate moss, although moss is never there.
Pushing this aside to get
under the floor, below the written, as
in a black winter pond, a cistern
or pipe or throat—
circling purple fish, shadow of an arm, toy boat—
voice thread thru stone, between the *s* and the *t* and the *one.*

to Rick Moody

ON (Dream)

Had then the dream *cash* (something persistent)
from bed to bed, unanchored
as from earth to fire to air
crash or *clash* or
the memory embodied in its shape
a man with gold portfolio
behind a wall, a villa, its shape
larger than "earth" or "water"
unattached to the sign at the side of the house
unattached to the dress
not the tiny bird on the long dark bough
calling *me me me*
not the plastic scissors (a cartoon)
great drift of ragweed
melody crouched under noise—
o thing, you cannot cradle this relic
as it travels thru what is.

THE RETURN OF WEATHER

The world is a double-storied mystery
and the unlucky link

found at the hotel
is as a nail in hell

missing an S.
Brave vestibule. The map

opens its pages to water.

        Which came first
        mercy or drowning?

        Dip the talisman in rain.
        Where, what message?

        Dissonant hiss—
        hot metal, splash—

        To market to market
        Ho hai! Ho hai!

        Into Persia they marched
        stitching pledge to pledge.

But the presently has no present
and the little while grows long.

Heavy storms
into incredulity torn

        fragments of the vessel

                    somber and unpeopled
        to the prow of an eminence
do not

        please do not
    so despicable a trifle
        a heave—

                        (Noise from the water
            a choir of shadows)

        an action
        fluted and winged

        a gray sequence
        puddled with

        dawn, a
        frayed green scarf

                        (something falls
                            darker than blindness)

each drop
scars the lens

and the spilling explosion
colorless, spinal, metallic

bruises the water
over light's impossible path.

The hill is laid out, its integer known. Climbing, we exchanged
glances over the future beneath us, lit up
and adapted. There was an idea, perhaps, in this
configuration. We fumbled with the keys and went into another room
whose shelves we trusted. You noticed stacks of envelopes,

photographs tacked to a wall. I noticed a tree in the window. A restless breeze
opened the lost letter, a want ad issued out over the plains.
But when the thing fell into the water we were afraid.

Please hold a space open, please
bring in the nets
a prophet's lost prayer
night's incendiary tale.

A body is missing.

Trade dinner for hot stones

evening for a gang
bending and bending

the slender grass
for a voice that is not your own.

Within such sorrows, assorted gleams
rushing toward sacrifice, a phrase
catches, a pocket of
pleasures
cartoons rapidly, so that whosoever witnessed is
brought to say *I am here* transpiring in its wake.
The storm is communal but far. Against
which already written extension, the supplicant
prays at the opening, breeding channels from spires, from a name
plots constancy, forms an alliance
with the deed.
Stories pour forth their cocoons of mist
even the ludicrous pasture, bony and vivid,
extends our way. With what fund or fountain were
we to proceed? Under the wooden mast, a small boat
traverses the page, a cloud
trails a blue floor, a bird

a bird cloud passes dumbly thru glass—

The captain fishes for scarecrows.

Strolling along the chronicle
a prophecy is summoned. I am sent
as agent and, even in such vagrancy,
change from image
to trace, tipped away from my place
in the hold—mercurial young god
thumping above, lilies upheld, words
curling up onto the neck's fever and rash—
opening near the figure where
he had been sleeping—

> *Palace of colors, angel merchant, the enchanted scene*
> *including a warehouse of braids and pink shoes. A flash and then a*
> *contraction into gold drops—the final incomparable descent into smithereens.*
> *Helped over the ditch and into the field while the thing kept receding under the*
> *raining dust, twisting in sleek air, elongated, the spectator, at the eastern or*
> *western end of the gallery, watches it disperse*

into what is
such as wind over a familiar face
and the bright disheveled stuff—petals or threads—

casting their way
along the threshold of consent

unless the soldier recants
over the thousands of bodies

unless the statue's tears of new blood
dry into rubies

unless the mast devolves to a tree,
the tree to a girl

One ration—*is this yours?*
One smile against the question—*yes.*
One risk—*it is raining again.*

STAIRCASE

Stay. A legible harmonic twins the harbor.
There are choral episodes
among the sails, and the kingfisher's plunge.
Stay. A petty wind fingers heat
like a girl her curls, gazing out
at the ensuing collision. A woman,
steering into floodwaters, is swept into a canyon
in Tucson, Arizona. Had she read Empedocles?
Had she recently wept? Light
infected leaves, then drab, then
heavily attired
the ephemera of air's
sway, window to window, like a disembodied
wing, its passage wholly unrecovered.
In mournful arousal
a flame cascades, as if to touch the end.
Something waits in the normal blue,
a Saturday, or love, or a city besieged.
The effects were known; they were the lived thing
ardently collapsing into a distant litter:
remote pages to be burned,
the wake of a small green boat
allotted to a scrim, or Paris,
or Celan. How beautiful, how untrue!
is what historians would say
as white stuff swept over the bow
not ever acknowledged—
not yet counted, not yet
found. There is
the ferret, Luna, lost in a woodpile
in the dog days of August.
Someone called Matthew, and someone called Tom,
move across time as across a bright lawn while

a felicity steers into moonlessness, where
one might say *not a matter of seeing,*
a matter of touch. Homer, for example,
finding his way down the staircase.

to Jonathan Schell

A HISTORY LESSON

Guardian memoir, elicit a last uncontaminated letter.
Pathos exceeds shanty exaltation.
One shade meets another, enlarging
the last lexicon
of perception, the grass roots phenomenon
listed in the last alphabet of song.
Saith the preacher, etc. *Beloved,* etc.
Harvest moon festival, everyone
out on the beach
with lanterns. She said *that is a theoretical color*
pointing at the garment on the wall, sleeves
knit from an old, perhaps the last, desire.
Meanwhile, a channel deports
humiliation as a form of
entertainment—man as dog,
woman as venomous master.
Rancid Night
staggers into a car
wearing lethal sequins,
flaunting her private parts. A hum
and the rustling of bags, details
crumbled into nail clippings and hair
between houshold plants.
There is a young boy
erect over a river, a girl with
maple syrup in her hair.
The day seems unfettered
but illusion bends down slowly
as the kingfisher rattles the air above a dying pond.
What is betrayal but a collision of belief with action.
Havel calls it ideology. Look it up: *exile, spirit in.*

DAYLIGHT SAVINGS TIME

Unimpeachable wilderness indicted; sagacious sea
at the herald stage, the stain of arrest.
The red berries are poisonous, the land
trembling with gaslight, muddied by glass.
Could this be forward? She knocks
at the frugal door as the train stops at the strand
averting a tragedy. This would be spectacle and so
a film would come out of the dusk
so that we are stranded with morning
tucked under the wreck, and the beloved voice
not anything anyone could hear. The iconic delusion
starts to cry real tears as she picks up the corpse and goes on.

But your voice has changed, and here is my favorite ghost
asleep in bed, in the midst of other bodies.
The throat—as if in memory of a friend—
empties itself under the roof
of the double roof. She lay in the tinsel light
grafted there, still as a doll,
and tried to say this word, this *garçon,* is not
the blond lad striding into malty night
at another's behest. Here I appear as my father's
worst dream, in which the opening to the tent
shifts into a riot of possibilities
and his sense of belonging is turned to a nomad's rite
set over the desert on a high plain. A ring of hair
is presented for good service, but he covets the sword
passed from one to another in a ceremony
with a figure at the helm, bejewelled and calm.
The linen frock she wore on the tennis court
was a prelude but it too
landed in the bin with rusty armpits
and buttons lost in a basket of lost buttons.

The dawn is too dark for words.
Obscurity is wanted like a ditch
out of which an embrace might be figured
the day we were lost in the woods
and waded thru muck at the edge
of an artificial lake
in the shape of a kiss, fish drawn on its sides, lilies
engraved on its surface.
I had forgotten my camera
so there is no evidence
and you have asked me not to tell.
Others are free
to imagine another story
flipped from pages of a book they intend some day to read.
It was only an imitation landscape and this still a draft
purloined from copies awaiting notation.
Too many names were dropped along the way
lint everywhere and you are invited to
a future as the doves
dip their tails in water and make their
noise. The day keeps raising stakes
and I thought how the particular could be nonpictorial
rising and falling like a conversation
instantly erased. *Hello, hello. Goodbye.*

DELAYED ELEGY

Young man, your mouth
belongs to an alphabet, the one
that starts near O and moves quickly on to
Q. This could be found in the diary, only
it would be after the X.
It would be after the X
which stymies passage, where only
shadows cross the threshold strung with lies.
The temporal would exist, then, because
the wind—what you never did say—would
let it fall into place like a tent for angels, or for what,
in such requisitions that angels come to make, we get to hear.

Already noon has dragged her riddle into view.
I have forgotten the answer.
Some malady in thin water,
island of lost fathers, returning ghosts with forgotten ties.
What the tongue does, it also undoes.
The deft hand on the wires or strings, remember?
A body hanging, a chair capsized.

AND THE QUESTION OF

(Note: most of the language culled from *Of Spirit: Heidegger and the Question* by Jacques Derrida, translated by Geoffrey Bennington and Rachel Bowley)

1.

What of this meantime?

In the name of
avoidance he forgot to avoid

entangled

          for example

the economy in those places

                 to approach, to make it appear

under a crossing out

        pneuma, spiritus, Geist

            (crouching enigma, cadaverous light)

under the title, under test
the *chora* in it.

        What is the knot, the single simple knot

at stake is the
collecting and gathering

why

         (method of embryonic toil, the daunting proposal
            of resilient cups, loped dashes,
                shattered and additive, the
                   radiant stains prior to us)

Is it already the question?

the call, the guarding

Is it still the question?

be patient here

pragma, praxis, pragmata

on the hand
in the domain of the hand
between speech and the hand
handwriting
the interpretation of the hand
of hand and animal

sheltered in obscurity manifest

the stone is without world
the animal is poor in world

now withdrawn   the examples of the chora

the ambiguous clarity

these four threads.

2.

A leap, a rupture

out of the question, out of the way

and, in silence,

(a thing, reality, thing-ness)

the I and reason
goes without saying

Now who are we?

We were speaking a moment ago of the question.

You cannot say that a stone is indifferent to its being without

I am, you are.

Not at all that of the stone or the tablet.

The stone is placed

before the difference, between indifference   *zu fragen*

the root of the who

the absolute indifference of the stone.

We will come back to this.

3.

On the horizon

a task, destiny or a further becoming.

I don't see, I do not know which—*spirit, soul, heart*—

yes and no.

Later (along

this path

a man and a woman

meet) we cannot go.

POEM WITH LAST LINE FROM EPICTETUS

Gray against further gray
her figure an allowance

walking along her own
counting or making sure

supplemental to what he might see
or to what he does see

looking out (below her)
gray against further, contiguous

sentence of plumes
the branches felled, the sway

specific pockets
where lovers spoon

woman with portrait of her son
and the other, the American,

in a war zone, upheaval of names
telling, unable to tell

so it is said *whosoever*
in an archive yet to come

evidence of what will be laid down
pasture, stone, the coastal hum

parade of dancers on Main Street
the adored who says *I am*

sky's ripening air
daily opulent rigor

bits of a body in time
my bit of a body, you mean.

HERE/THIS/THERE/THAT

Move back, figure, into the hoop.
Demonstrate, famished as it is,
the meagre, crumbled
chew of a step onto snow.
An arch lifts from the shadow's range
and tilts, coming up to away: a limit.

And the one said
are these folded or are they extended
out of all or any sighting?
I have awakened to their stamina.
Description as symptom,
radiant throat between this one and that.

A vase, a lamp, a curtain, a door
             va la ta do
sings the echo,
its restive partial connection
frayed. Voice follows sound
as if wanting so to perch.
A stamped certain floor.
Logistics of the melted appraisal
two, three, four,
slight grammar of drop and thing.

Hosts and guests. I have awakened
among celebrants, singing
and bowing.
Neither shade nor echo, an upheaval
unnumbered: crowd? storm? chorus?
Here I now, here I now,
and then *Now I hear.*
Retrieved from where?
From what follows what lasts.

AUCTION

What is a day?
A jailed man in a dream's revision
and an aged woman
that old hag
drums on the soundboard of a piano
glad to be dead. Chocolate kisses
on glass plates, O.J.'s trial,
investigations into the telling
of the told. A clown looks down
at his belly, the icicle's long tooth drips,
light falls apart on the snow lathed ground.
An old rich man marries a young woman
and another, slow with girth,
drives back and forth in a red car
distracted by the particulars of what is not yet appraised.

What am I offered for
this day? For the jailed man
in the dream's revision,
for the ghost at the piano, candy kisses, plates,
what for news in its dailiness?
The clown is a procedural error, not for sale.
The red car is leased, as is the snow enhanced ground.

Rapidly, as in the subject of a theft,
a task ricochets uphill,
the man there waiting, the woman violent,
distance in ruined recompense,
its return to the diction
of having been, owning its limit, its usual address,
and I in my late habits, my lovers secret, my delays known,
(offset by the joke I do not know to tell)
I who have arrived at the pinion of a twig,

who have not yet opened,
my hat and my polka–dot pants, painted lashes,
eyes wide set, I who have been
asleep at the bottom of the page
awaiting the festive,
put down my bid: as yet unspent gain.

ON

What could be seen from this angle
a hinge, thin shell
of thought
            Outside: the simple vocabulary
betrayal and fact

or perhaps a shelf without shine
recently built

(binding, looseleaf)

the city's opulent announcement
its conjuring trick

Old women should be explorers?
I'll be an Indian, already risen, already insulted.

How does that song go? *You've got to be taught.*

N/EST

In that part of the day I was carefully measured for aridity

whether or not it had rained, the air plummeting with hellish weeping, the hairy
leaves on the maple by the pond, under which Phillip had wed Cynthia, shaped like
a child's balloon or a pregnant woman, almost round but with a gash delved into its
midst, turned back, thrashing, into silvery green, so I am reminded of my mother
bending over, her wet hair falling across her upside-down face, brushing brushing
the long tawny length of it

                        not under my arms but elsewhere, around
the wrists and ankles and fingernails where you wouldn't expect to find
moisture ordinarily

              and at other times, around midday, when the kids are all
at the pool but Yo-Yo continues to bark with a high piercing yip yip in great
despair and no matter how many windows I close the sound

Helping Julia to pack for California, wrapping her dishes in old newspaper, placing
them in a beautiful old salad bowl, taking them out to her car to place in an open
trunk, barefoot, in the muggy heat of July, that day, while her son Adam sat on the
camp bed and read, the bees came like tiny bombs

I was seven, in Bridgehampton, where we had a small white house down by the
pond, white lilies opened only in the morning, and I went out into the thick
mud where there were bloodsuckers, and picked one or two to give to my father,
who was asleep inside the house, but when I came up the slope, my legs all
muddied, the bees

      I thought I was being

                punished

                          later he died
                          September

of polio just before my birthday these days
twist into one

tripped on a rug and in my dream
he is leaving on a train
I am lifted up in an envelope

                                    the white sky reflected thru the trees in the pond

I took a photograph
her daughter Isobel standing in the pond, her shadow
elongated in the water, braided hair a gold shimmer
her solitude

looking back over the past five months
I forgot to read *Moby-Dick* and now it is too late

                    I thought the world was held by language as if it were an
                                        incipience

Late at night reading Michael Ondaatje's *The English Patient:*

*"There was a time when mapmakers named the places they travelled through with
the names of lovers rather than their own. Someone seen bathing in a desert caravan,
holding up muslin with one arm in front of her. Some old Arab poet's woman, whose
white-dove shoulders made him describe an oasis with her name. The skin bucket
spreads water over her, she wraps herself in the cloth, and the old scribe turns from
her to describe Zerzura."*

        My father
                                        traveled during the war and wrote
                                        his name was Richard, called Dick
Childlessness
        brings estrangement

            I have never explicitly affiliated my not having children with

my father's absences
I thought I would find him in the heavy
book of words, dictionary
which rested on his writing table long after his
disappearance and which I thought
was magical, containing all secrets,

or perhaps
find a way to him on little word boats, paper sails, some spirit's breath,
into a "conversation," Paul Celan's term—

This turn, this coming about, refuses to let time go, but is always using it to

fuel the poem towards the meaning of
the presence of meaning

I have been pregnant three times

two abortions while in college, one in Milwaukee
without anesthetic after which I bled

in the Emergency Room I was afraid they would send me to jail
I told my English teacher
who had said *I don't know if you have ever thought about it, but
you can write*
seeding my life with pursuit

Fred, the father, died last year in New Mexico.
We were engaged. He gave me a
ring, a small emerald set in diamonds, at the end of the summer
in Santa Fe.
I had been working as a mother's helper in New Jersey taking care
of three children, their mother pregnant with her fourth

the youngest, Pete, called my name each morning had

immense glee
learning a word for a thing *bird? bird?* hearing one sing

after she went to the hospital to give birth
her husband came into my room
filled with moonlight

I remember thinking *what what what*

Fred wrote *"come out on a hobby horse I will still love you"*
We drove to Second Mesa to watch the Hopi Snake Dance
a gaggle of Indian children surrounded us
calling him Mr. Smokestack laughing I bought a tiny clay dish
with a creature painted on it

he showed me the desert

married an English girl they had three children. When he died the marriage had
collapsed. When he drank he talked too much, brilliance becoming garrulous,
sentimental, pretentious. I kept his letters. I thought he was smarter than anyone
in the world when I was seventeen. He had read Nietzsche and Céline, nihilist
in the midst of idealists. He called me "Little Chick." He encouraged me to write.

*"In the desert the most loved waters, like a lover's name, are carried blue in your
hands, enter your throat. One swallows absence."*

The second time

was an accident
studying for exams all night
it was lovely exhausted sex
I have forgotten his name

the word *name* has *man* and *men* in it

Ondaatje writes of his heroine Hana: *"To rest was to receive all aspects of the world without judgement. A bath in the sea, a fuck with a soldier who never knew your name. Tenderness towards the unknown and anonymous, which was a tenderness to the self."*

                    I flew to Puerto Rico/pretended to be going to a wedding
spent the night in a nasty airport motel the man there tried to
come on to me/could not sleep/fluorescent dawn all night

                    my first trip out of the United States

            I took a taxi to the place/there were stairs
                        along the outside of the building
                                    walking up them/I imagined a film set

my stomach was upset
they sent me to get Pepto-Bismol
the doctor had gold chains around his neck, his shirt open

the nurse a large kind woman/many had their boyfriends with them
everyone paid in cash
                                    one woman was reading *Steal This Book*
I was awake they spoke Spanish
numb down from my waist
watching his face/hearing the scrapes

afterwards at another motel
                            sunshine and blue water amazed
                                    to be alive
                        it was the middle of winter in the midwest

pretended I was on vacation/dark glasses and a hat
reading Henry James' *The Wings of the Dove*
alone in the restaurant/I kept inventing
a substitute self

80

The third time years later
I was already scheduled for a hysterectomy
fibroid uterine tumors

and then told I was pregnant I talked to various
doctors about the pregnancy they said the fetus is not viable premature babies are
very costly I had no insurance working part-time in a gallery Brian was trying to
figure out how to be an artist in New York

his daughter, Haven, eight when we met she is married now in Boston
I do not hear from her sometimes I see Brian on the street

Phillip and Cynthia's daughter is now fifteen she was in Paris modeling/I have
almost never seen her smile/her beauty is

the subject's object
the object's subject

eyes traps of green light
limbs long limber new branches

lawn after rain

swimming in the pool, the photographer walking round and round
his camera wheezing and clicking

hawk circling the blue sky above
inscribing a dangerous

I walked up and down in the kitchen with her crying in my arms
she was five months old/I said
she is angry
not to speak

does not speak to me thinks I do not like kids because I like to
revision the silence/or because

on the street she is
wearing a black wig short skirt bright red lipstick high heels walking with her father
she says the wig is hot/in the photos she is barely recognizable as herself
they have made her up

        her mother asked me when I first was interested in becoming
part of the country co-op if I intended to have children this struck me as an
odd question

        then I went into the hospital
for the operation but the last minute it was decided that they would do a D&C, an
official abortion, rather than risk the hysterectomy because when you are pregnant
your blood is "frothy" so I was sent home to wait
wept ceaselessly

        an image of a cork on a sea

I saw it on a gray screen
tiny incoherent scribble
don't you want this baby the nurse asked/she did not understand

        and then I went back
    they put me to sleep
        I woke up cold
          gray as dry ice

    I went out with Phillip a few times a long time ago he was
        handsome and intense I was a waitress then in SoHo

and then went back
for another surgery to remove
my ovaries
     had become
        an explosion of impossible life
         teeth hair brainmatter
          homunculus
           ubiquitous

                    the scar revisits
                              is its is its
                                        sealed shut
                    time's incubus

Space here is
always shifting/birds
sparrows catbirds chickadees robins the cedar waxwings
love the cherry tree/a great swarm of blackbirds came over the house/a wind of
dark flight/they make a *cluck* sound land deep in the foliage

across the pond
a hermit thrush/partial lament
a blue heron in a dead gray tree
the belted kingfisher's rattle
before it plummets

there is no word for the sound
a splash is

                                        Each choice
          measures the relation between freedom and fate

Emerson writes, *"Where do we find ourselves? In a series of which we do not know
the extremes, and believe that it has none. We wake and find ourselves on a stair;
there are stairs belows us, which we seem to have ascended; there are stairs above us,
many a one, which go upward and out of sight."*

These steps I took
I do not regret

                    to be a poet

they were illegal dangerous
sad and expensive

is a constant iteration of choice
one word instead of another
they call to each other sometimes/constructing a place

in which to live a life

words are acts of the world they are prior to us
issued forth
they become facts in the world
an address

Nan comes to visit she is pregnant
her son Henry

is born four flights below

the place where
I watched Joe die/the machine screamed at his last breath

the rufous sparrows nested in the blue spruce/listening
a tiny fledgling came out on a low branch Sylvia came to get me she said
it looked like Albert Einstein with big eyebrows and a large beak I took its picture it
stared mutely at the camera I said it looked like her husband Mike

their daughter Jane, just fifteen, broke up with her first boyfriend
she was so sad I have a picture of her at three in a pink bathing suit

when poems are made I try to listen to how they want to become
sometimes they perish

later it disappeared

in the photograph a blur on a bough of blue spruce
the nest a palm of dry mud on the ground.

INVOCATION

Speak, Mistress Quaker, a parable waits from which
blessings issue, conditionally, as in a hunt, a possible hearing
wherein the manifest flirts, beguiling, almost at home.
Speak on, Troubled Specter, as in a calm
carefree silence whose message embraces its
quick. Seed that, so
the trail is viable, literal, glad
as in love's timing: tick-tock luck.
A siege of incipient cures! A brevity so enhanced
the Pilgrim finds her way along the path of red berries
through the wild into the dilated Spot where following ends and begins
and ends again. *You were in a tale,* a choice you had not made,
whose dim constellation gathers dew on the sleeve of hours,
the iteration of just cause, saving one against the others, as in a court.
Be kind, Mistress of Woes, Hooligan of Ages. Be a Treaty we sign.
Chafe against brittle nudity, swallow the excellent potion, remain among thieves.
Remain among thieves, steal Advent from avarice, dark from idiot sight.

to Bernadette Mayer

ABOUT THE AUTHOR

Ann Lauterbach is the author of five collections of poetry, including *And For Example* and *Clamor* (both Penguin). She lives in New York, where she is a professor at The City College and Graduate Center; she is also a director of writing in the M.F.A. program at Bard College. In 1993, she was a recipient of a MacArthur fellowship.

PENGUIN POETS

Paul Beatty	*Joker, Joker, Deuce*
Ted Berrigan	*Selected Poems*
Philip Booth	*Pairs*
Jim Carroll	*Fear of Dreaming*
Nicholas Christopher	*5° & Other Poems*
Carl Dennis	*Ranking the Wishes*
Stuart Dischell	*Evenings and Avenues*
Stephen Dobyns	*Common Carnage*
Paul Durcan	*A Snail in My Prime*
Amy Gerstler	*Crown of Weeds*
Amy Gerstler	*Nerve Storm*
Debora Greger	*Desert Fathers, Uranium Daughters*
Robert Hunter	*Glass Lunch*
Robert Hunter	*Sentinel*
Jack Kerouac	*Book of Blues*
Ann Lauterbach	*And For Example*
Ann Lauterbach	*Clamor*
Ann Lauterbach	*On a Stair*
Derek Mahon	*Selected Poems*
Michael McClure	*Three Poems*
Carol Muske	*An Octave Above Thunder*
Alice Notley	*The Descent of Alette*
Anne Waldman	*Kill or Cure*
Robert Wrigley	*In the Bank of Beautiful Sins*